This book is about the builders of the pyramid of Senwosret I.
Senwosret was the son of Amenemhat I.
Senwosret built many monuments during his long reign.
He ruled Egypt from 1918 to 1875 B.C.
His son Amenemhat II ruled from 1876 to 1842 B.C.

Montuhotep was one of Senwosret's most important officials.
He served Senwosret as treasurer and was later
promoted to chief minister, overseeing the building and
completion of the pyramid.

We don't know the names of the other people who built the
pyramid, but the names used in the book have been taken from
people who lived at that time, doing these kinds of jobs.

The book is based on the published research
of Dieter and Dorothea Arnold of
The Metropolitan Museum of Art in New York.

Dr. Richard Parkinson at the Department of Egyptian
Antiquities at the British Museum was the consultant.

For Rachel M. H.

For Elliott & Cameron R. H-B.

Text copyright © 2001 by Meredith Hooper
Illustrations copyright © 2001 by Robin Heighway-Bury
Illustrations pp. 32–36 copyright © 2001 by Walker Books Ltd.
Hieroglyphs p. 37 and p. 38 copyright © by Dr. Richard Parkinson

Edited by Jackie Gaff, Camilla Hallinan, and Paul Harrison
Designed by Beth Aves
Illustrations pp. 32–36 by Mike Bostock

First U.S. edition 2001

Library of Congress Cataloging-in-Publication Data

Hooper, Meredith.
Who built the pyramid? / Meredith Hooper ;
[illustrated by] Robin Heighway-Bury. — 1st U.S. ed.
p. cm.
ISBN 0-7636-0786-X
1. Pyramids — Egypt — Juvenile literature. [1. Pyramids — Egypt.
2. Egypt — Antiquities.] I. Heighway-Bury, Robin, ill.
DT63.H66 2001
932'.013 — dc21   00-066730

2 4 6 8 10 9 7 5 3 1

Printed in Italy

This book was typeset in Rusticana, Myriad Tilt, and Egyptienne.
The illustrations were done on computer.

Candlewick Press
2067 Massachusetts Avenue
Cambridge, Massachusetts 02140

visit us at www.candlewick.com

THE LAND WAS GIVEN TO ME,
ITS LENGTH AND BREADTH;
I HAVE BEEN NURSED AS A
BORN CONQUEROR. THE LAND
WAS GIVEN TO ME; I AM ITS
LORD. MY POWER HAS REACHED
THE HEIGHTS OF HEAVEN △

A building text of Senwosret I, 1915 B.C.

WHO BUILT

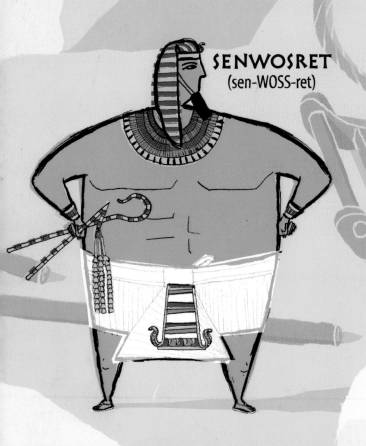

SENWOSRET
(sen-WOSS-ret)

MONTUHOTEP
(mon-too-HOE-tep)

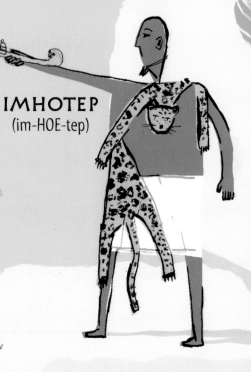

IMHOTEP
(im-HOE-tep)

NAKHT
(nakt)

WAH
(wah)

NESUMONTU
(ness-oo-MON-too)

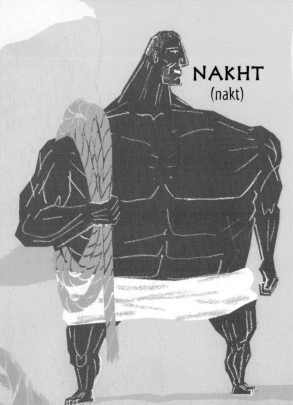

THE PYRAMID?

AMENEMHAT
(ah-men-EM-hot)

SENEBU
(SEN-eh-boo)

AMENY
(AH-men-ee)

INYOTEF
(in-YOE-teff)

MEREDITH HOOPER

illustrated by
ROBIN
HEIGHWAY-BURY

SASOBEK
(sa-SO-beck)

CANDLEWICK PRESS
CAMBRIDGE, MASSACHUSETTS

I DID, SAID SENWOSRET.

With the lift of an eyebrow. With a word of command.

I am king of all Egypt. What I say happens.

My power reaches to the heights of heaven.

I built the pyramid as my tomb. After I die,

I shall lie beneath it, with my treasures around me.

My name will be remembered for all eternity.

I BUILT THE PYRAMID.

SAID MONTUHOTEP.

With my understanding of the king.

I am his chief minister.

Nothing happens without my knowing it.

Nothing is done without my ordering it.

I designed the pyramid so that

it would last forever.

I decided where to hide His Majesty's

burial chamber, deep underground.

I do as my king wishes.

△

I BUILT THE PYRAMID.

I DID, SAID IMHOTEP.

With my secret knowledge

and my secret learning.

I am the high priest of all Egypt.

It was I who chose where to build the pyramid.

It was I who calculated exactly

the direction it must face.

△

I BUILT THE PYRAMID.

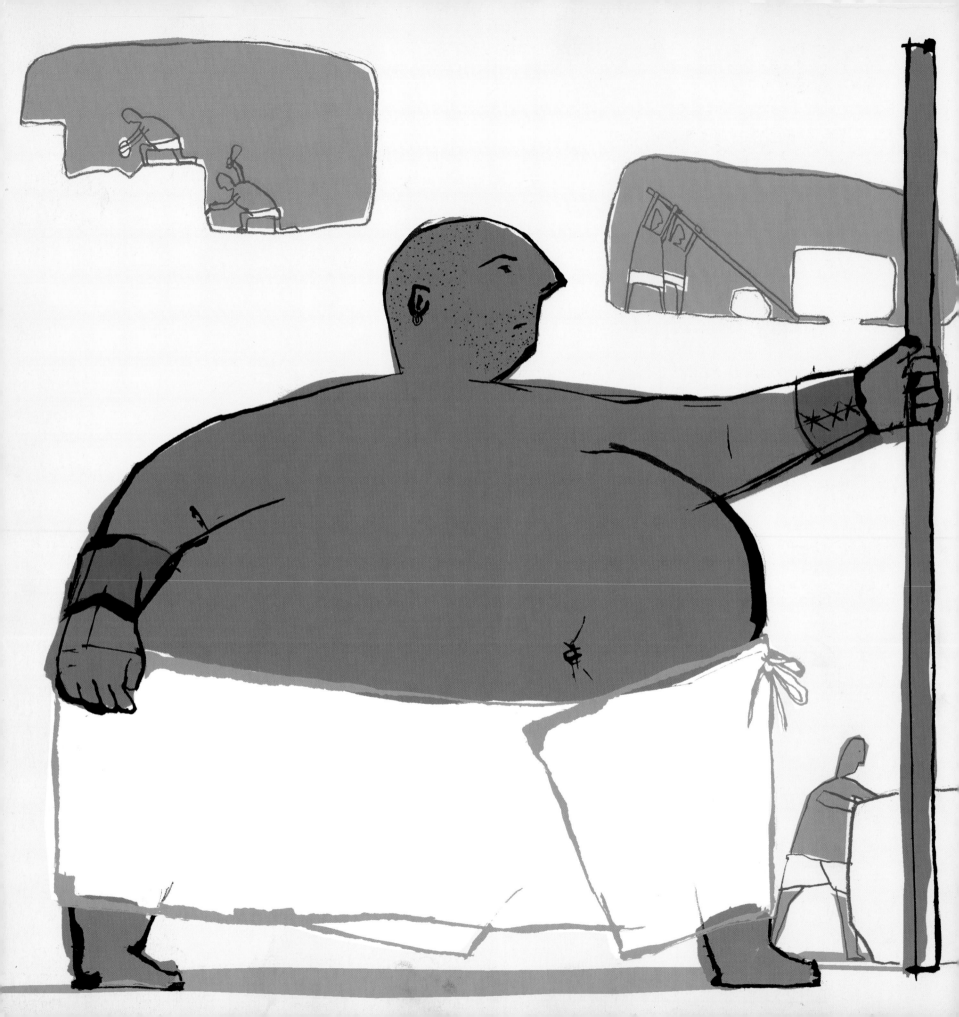

I DID,
SAID SENEBU.

With my experience,

thirty years of experience.

I'm the quarry master, the best in all Egypt.

I knew where to find the stones to build the pyramid.

Hard granite from far off in the desert.

Fine white limestone from across the Nile.

There's no pyramid without stones.

IT'S OBVIOUS.

I BUILT THE PYRAMID.

I DID, SAID AMENY.

With my know-how.

Me, old Ameny, the foreman of the gangs.

I knew how to hack through rock,

how to tunnel deep underground.

I cut out the place where His Majesty will lie

—life, prosperity, health to him!

Me. Old Ameny.

△

I BUILT THE
PYRAMID.

15

With my muscles and sweat,

with blisters and aching bones.

Me and the other laborers.

We dragged the stones to the building site.

We pulled them up the ramps.

We pushed them into place on the pyramid.

WORK, WORK, WORK!

That's all I did.

I BUILT THE PYRAMID.

I DID, SAID WAH.

With my two tired legs.

With my two worn feet.

I'm the water carrier.

I carried water from a canal up to the building site.

Every day, in the hot sun, over the hot sand.

So many people needed water.

Without me, no one could get their work done.

Me, and my donkey.

△

I BUILT THE PYRAMID.

I DID, SAID NESUMONTU.

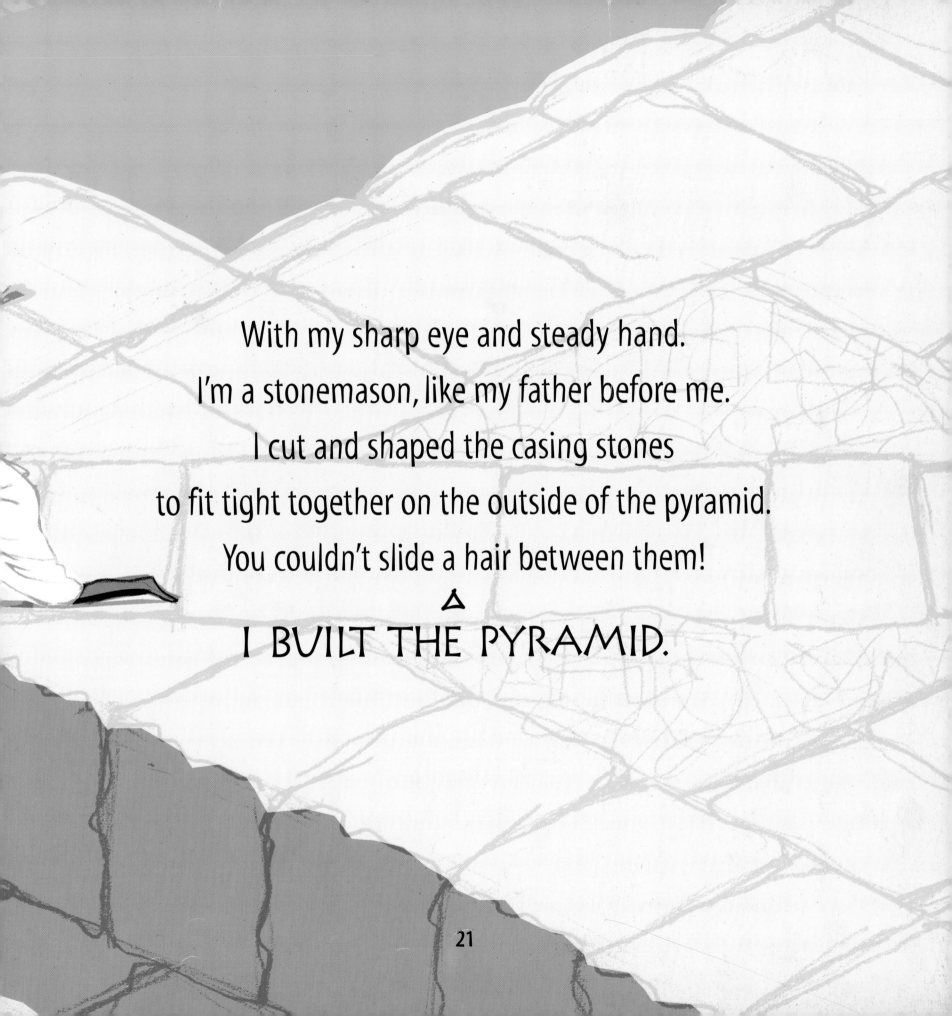

With my sharp eye and steady hand.
I'm a stonemason, like my father before me.
I cut and shaped the casing stones
to fit tight together on the outside of the pyramid.
You couldn't slide a hair between them!

I BUILT THE PYRAMID.

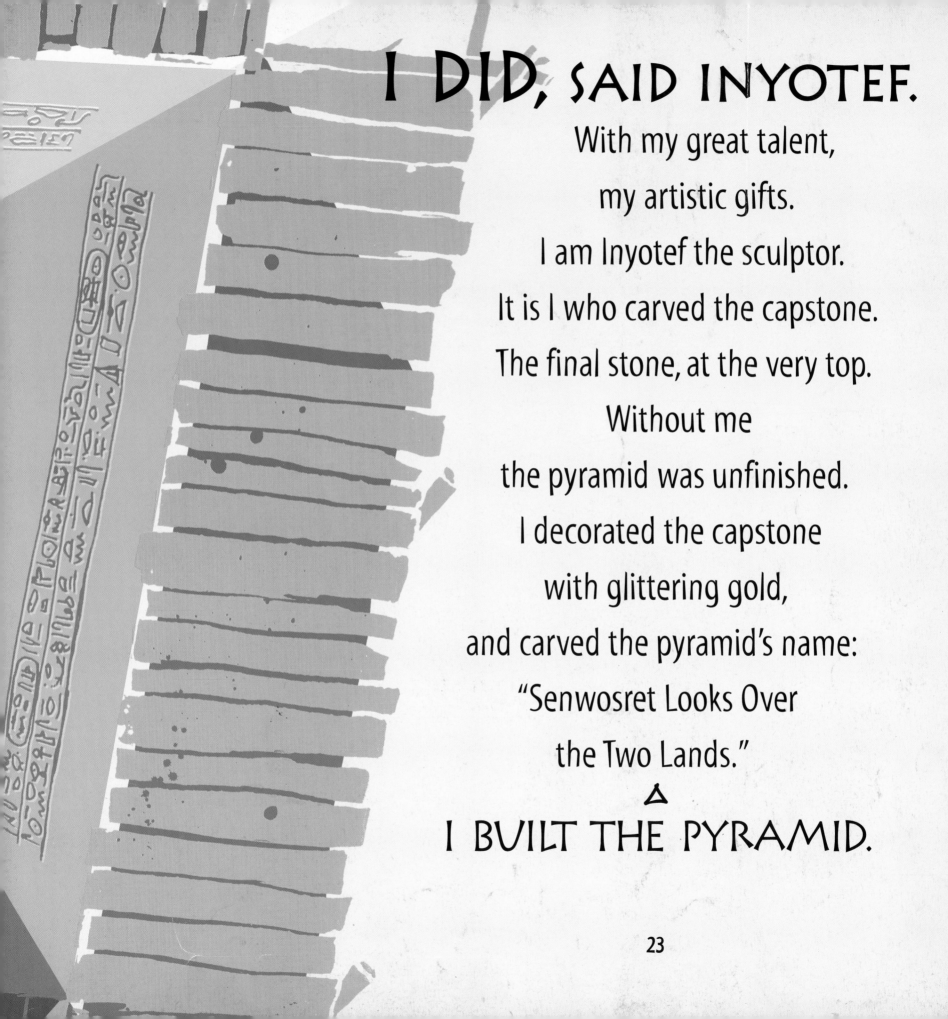

I DID, SAID INYOTEF.

With my great talent,

my artistic gifts.

I am Inyotef the sculptor.

It is I who carved the capstone.

The final stone, at the very top.

Without me

the pyramid was unfinished.

I decorated the capstone

with glittering gold,

and carved the pyramid's name:

"Senwosret Looks Over

the Two Lands."

△

I BUILT THE PYRAMID.

I DID, SAID

AMENEMHAT.

With the lift of an eyebrow.
With a word of command.
I am the new king of all Egypt.
I saw my father Senwosret's body
placed in his burial chamber. Then,
I ordered the burial chamber to be sealed,
forever. I blocked the secret passage that led
to the burial chamber, and hid its entrance.
I completed the work.

△

I BUILT THE PYRAMID.

WHO BUILT THE

SAID SASOBEK.

Me and my tomb robbers,

we tunneled down in the cramped airless dark.

Hard, sweaty, secret work.

We found the king's burial chamber.

We stole everything worth stealing.

All those others,

so what if they built the pyramid!

I KNEW HOW
TO GET IN.

Deep under Senwosret's pyramid the robbers,

in their cramped tunnel, wanted to get out, fast.

They dropped a few pieces of treasure in their hurry.

A golden dagger sheath. A few alabaster containers.

Bits of wooden boxes.

YEARS PASSED. Priests were no longer living in the temple buildings at the great pyramid.

Local people began breaking into the site. They pried off carvings and decorations, pulled away the fine polished casing stones covering the walls. They treated the pyramid and its buildings as a useful quarry.

The pyramid was sagging in any case, sinking under its own weight. Slowly the pyramid began to collapse. Relentlessly the wind and weather worked at the stones, wearing them, bit by bit. Cracking them in the sun's heat, the cold of the desert night.

Today Senwosret's pyramid is a pile of sand and rubble just over a third of its once great height.

Senwosret wanted his pyramid to last forever. It hasn't. It has decayed, like everything else.

The pyramid of Senwosret I as it looks today.

Lisht South Pyramid Courtesy: The Metropolitan Museum of Art, New York.

The view from Senwosret's pyramid toward his father Amenemhat's pyramid and the valley beyond.

THE FIRST archaeologists at the site of Senwosret's pyramid found the robbers' tunnel and the dropped pieces of treasure. They excavated the secret passage beneath the pyramid until near the bottom they were stopped by water. That was over 100 years ago.

Today, archaeologists working on the pyramid calculate that they have gotten within eight yards of Senwosret's burial chamber. But they cannot get through the final section of wet, sand-filled passage. Deep beneath the pyramid, the water level has been rising and the burial chamber is now flooded.

Every burial chamber in every Egyptian pyramid was broken into by robbers. But Senwosret's burial chamber was robbed only once. No one has entered it since. No one today knows what the burial chamber looks like, or if anything remains inside.

ARCHAEOLOGISTS from The Metropolitan Museum of Art in New York have found out a great deal about what Senwosret I's pyramid looked like, who built it and how. They sift through the heaps of rubble, the buried fragments, piecing together the evidence.

Stonemasons cut and smoothed the bottom and one side of each casing stone at the stone-dressing station.

This dotted line shows where the outer wall will be built.

Strong ramps built of brick, mud, and rubble sloped up onto the pyramid itself.

This dotted line shows where the inner wall will be built.

Yard for storing granite, close to the entrance of the secret passage.

Storage yard for limestone quarried from nearby hills.

Blocks of stone were marked with information like the name of the quarry, the dates of transport, route, when they were delivered to the storage area, and when they were dragged to the pyramid.

Mud bricks made next to the Nile were stored here.

Good wide roads were made of wooden beams buried in mortar and limestone chippings, sealed with Nile mud.

Brick buildings were used for site officials, workshops, and to store tools, but we don't know their exact position.

Storage yard for Tura limestone.

Roads and ramps leading to local limestone quarries.

Archaeologists have not found the site of the royal city or the canal that would have led from the Nile River, but they were to the east of the pyramid.

The road leading down to the quay where the Tura limestone was unloaded as rough blocks.

CONSTRUCTION Site of SENWOSRET'S PYRAMID

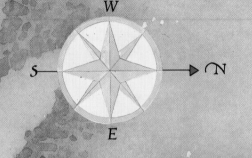

Granite was used for building the burial chamber, lining the secret passage, and for the great plugs to block the passage.

The workmen's camp was probably in the valley between the pyramids of Senwosret and Amenemhat 1.

Road to the quay where granite was unloaded.

Archaeologists are not sure exactly how the workmen lifted the stones two hundred feet up the side of the pyramid. Some of the stones weighed more than a ton.

Archaeologists don't know exactly where the workshops of carpenters, metalworkers, and potters were.

The COMPLETE PYRAMID Site

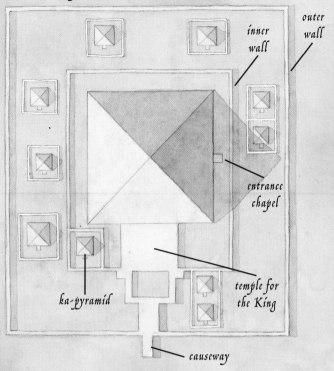

inner wall

outer wall

entrance chapel

temple for the King

ka-pyramid

causeway

Nine small pyramids were built, probably for Senwosret's queens, and a small ka-pyramid for Senwosret's spirit. There was an entrance chapel, a temple for the King, a causeway, and another temple down in the valley. An inner wall with life-sized carved and painted figures of fat offering-bearers surrounded the pyramid, with an outer wall beyond.

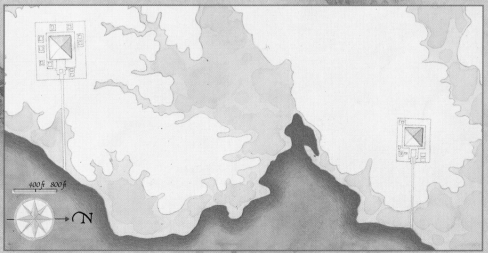

The site seen from above. Senwosret's pyramid left, Amenemhat's pyramid right.

ENWOSRET began to plan his pyramid as soon as he came to power. The pyramid of his father, Amenemhat I, was the first in Egypt for nearly 200 years. Amenemhat reunited Egypt and built a new capital city by the Nile River. Senwosret wanted his pyramid to be bigger and better than his father's. It was his royal tomb and he wanted it to last forever.

Senwosret believed that after he died he would live again. But his new life depended on everything being done correctly when he died and afterward. His body, with all the things he needed in his life after death, had to be kept safe so that his spirit could achieve new life, surrounded by his every requirement.

〰〰〰〰〰〰〰〰〰〰

The pyramid of Senwosret I was built 4,000 years ago during the Middle Kingdom. Senwosret I ruled for 43 years from 1918 to 1875 B.C. This statue comes from the pyramid site and is now in the Egyptian Museum, Cairo.

△

MONTUHOTEP was Senwosret's Chief Minister. He was in charge of the royal architects who designed Senwosret's pyramid. He planned the work. He gave

PA Jürgen Liepe

A plan of the internal walls of the pyramid. The thirty-two spaces between the walls were filled with big slabs of roughly shaped stones.

〰〰〰〰

the orders. The pyramid was to be built in a completely new way. A framework of huge, thick walls inside the pyramid would give it strength, like the skeleton in a body. There were no doors, passages, or rooms. The King's body would lie safe, deep beneath a solid mountain of stone.

△

IMHOTEP, as high priest, was in charge of the pyramid. Egyptians believed their king was a god, so the pyramid was also a temple. Imhotep chose a dramatic site for Senwosret's pyramid on a desert hilltop, close to his father's pyramid, beyond the royal city

In the great night sky, Imhotep could see a group of stars circling in the north, always visible. They were called the "Imperishable Ones." The secret passage, rising from the burial chamber like a pathway to the distant stars, had to face due north. So must Senwosret's burial chamber and coffin.

Imhotep laid out the huge square shape of the pyramid in the sand, facing exactly north, south, east, and west.

Most of the stones needed to build the pyramid could be quarried nearby. But the limestone for the casing stones came from Tura, and the granite for the burial vault came from Aswan.

∧∧∧∧∧∧∧∧∧∧∧∧∧∧∧∧∧∧

Four deep foundation pits were dug, one in each corner of the pyramid square. Then Imhotep held a foundation ceremony. Priests put offerings in each pit — birds, animals, clay pots, and bricks with the name of the pyramid. Now building could begin.

∧∧∧∧∧∧∧∧∧∧∧∧∧∧∧∧∧∧

Archaeologist's photograph of the offerings uncovered in one of the foundation pits.

MEDITERRANEAN SEA

LOWER EGYPT

× Tura

× Lisht ~ site of Senwosret's pyramid

River Nile

UPPER EGYPT

N

W   E

S

Aswan ×

GANGS of workmen dug a shaft in the center of the pyramid square, hacking through solid limestone. A deep pit for the king's burial chamber was cut out of the rock at the bottom. Beyond the northern edge of the pyramid, more gangs dug a sloping ramp down toward the central shaft. Basket boys toiled up it, carrying away waste rock.

When the burial chamber was finished, the shaft and sloping tunnel were filled in and the ground leveled. A new, narrow, sloping passage was hacked through the rock, above the old construction tunnel: the secret entrance to the burial chamber. It would be used only once, to carry the king's body to his final resting place.

Perhaps two thousand laborers worked on the construction site for two or four months at a time. Then they went back home to their villages to work in the fields again, while other laborers took their place.

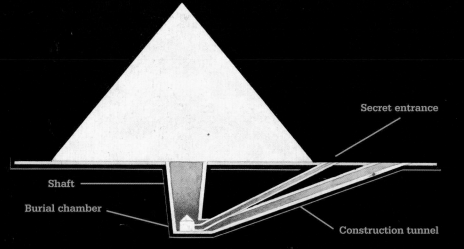

Senwosret's pyramid was 200 feet high and each side was 345 feet long.

Secret entrance

Shaft

Burial chamber

Construction tunnel

While the pyramid was being built its true shape could not be seen. It was hidden by ramps, roads, debris — all the mess of the construction site. But underneath, the four enormous triangular faces of Senwosret's pyramid had to rise with exactly the same slope, so that their tops came together, with no mistakes.

At the very top, a granite capstone was fitted into place, an exact miniature of the pyramid below. It was the only decorated stone on the whole pyramid. Eyes were carved on it as if Senwosret were looking out from inside, over his land.

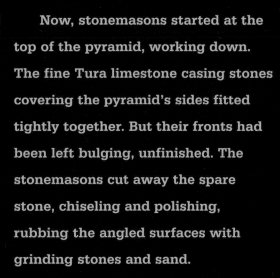

Senwosret's capstone has not been found, but it probably looked like this capstone from the pyramid of Amenemhat III now in the Egyptian Museum, Cairo.

Werner Forman Archive Egyptian Museum, Cairo

Now, stonemasons started at the top of the pyramid, working down. The fine Tura limestone casing stones covering the pyramid's sides fitted tightly together. But their fronts had been left bulging, unfinished. The stonemasons cut away the spare stone, chiseling and polishing, rubbing the angled surfaces with grinding stones and sand.

The true pyramid began to glare and shine.

Senwosret's pyramid was the biggest and highest built in Egypt for 500 years. Perhaps 5,000 quarrymen, masons, laborers, and other workmen — specialists, as well as support staff — were needed to build it.

An enormous amount of material was used: thousands of basketloads of sand from the desert; thousands of moulds filled with Nile mud, to make bricks; thousands of trees to make tools, sledges, boats, to burn for fuel, to cook food; tens of thousands of jars of water; around a quarter of a million stones — limestone and granite, alabaster, dolerite and quartzite; continuous supplies for meals — bread and beer, vegetables and fish.

Building the pyramid was a massive task. It happened because of the countless repetition of jobs by vast numbers of people. The pyramid of Senwosret I looked magnificent when it was finished. It probably took twenty years to build.

SON OF THE SUN GOD: SENWOSRET, MAY HE LIVE FOR ALL TIME AND ETERNITY.

INDEX

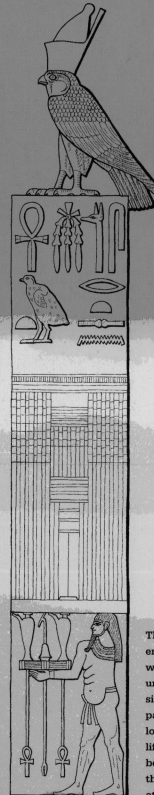

The high inner wall enclosing the pyramid was decorated in unique style on both sides with carved and painted panels. Two long processions of life-size offering-bearers move around the pyramid, ending at the temple of the King, Senwosret I.

MEREDITH HOOPER

uses the storybook form in *Who Built the Pyramid?* to make the latest research accessible for a young audience. A historian by training, Meredith Hooper is the author of many books ranging in subject from Antarctica to aviation, from the history of water to the history of inventions.

ROBIN HEIGHWAY-BURY

has been illustrating for sixteen years but this is his first book for children. Robin Heighway-Bury lives in London, and found inspiration for his illustrations for *Who Built the Pyramid?* at the Egyptian galleries at the British Museum, which is just a short distance from his studio.